Stories in this book

BIBLE GAMES

2018 Colin Tinsley

ISBN 978-1-909751-86-6

Published by

www.hopeforyouthministries.org

Colin Tinsley
6 Hawthorn Hill, Kinallen, Dromore,
Co. Down, BT25 2HY, Northern Ireland
Email hopeforyouthministries@gmail.com
Web www.hopeforyouthministries.org

1. Playing in the Sand

As a little boy, I loved playing in the sand. It was so soft to run in and play with. Building sandcastles was always a favourite thing to do at the seaside. I used to love running along the beach, doing handstands and all sorts of things that children love to do.

In the Bible we read that God spoke to Abraham and told him he would have as many children as there were stars in the sky or just like the grains of sand on the seashore. What did He mean by this?

God was not referring to physical sons and daughters but rather children of faith. That is people who believe in God - those who have asked the Lord Jesus Christ to be their Saviour and by faith become born-again Christians. God was foretelling that there would be millions of Christians - more than anyone could ever count; just like the grains of sand on the seashore.

Sand was also mentioned in the Bible when Jesus was teaching the people using a parable. The story was about two men - a wise man and a foolish man. One of the men built his house upon a rock but the other man built his house upon the sand. Which man do you think was wise and which one do you think was foolish?

Both houses looked really well when they were finished. However, when a storm came and the wind blew on both houses, the one built on a rock stood firm but the one built on sand fell to pieces! Why do you think this happened?

The house built on sand fell because it did not have a firm foundation. The foundation of a house may not be visible when the house is finished but it is the most important part of the building. No one has ever seen God, yet He is the most important person in the universe.

Just like a house needs a strong foundation, our lives need to be built upon the Lord Jesus Christ. When He is our foundation and life

becomes tough, we know that He is always there to protect us from falling.

1. **When God told Abraham about having as many children as there were grains of sand on the seashore, what did He mean?**

2. What happens when you build your house on the sand?

3. **What happens when you build your house on a rock?**

4. How can we build our lives upon the Lord Jesus Christ?

5. **When is the best time to build our lives upon the Lord Jesus Christ?**

PRAYER...

Dear Lord, it is fascinating that we can build our lives upon You. It makes sense as You care for us so much. Help me not to make mistakes like the foolish man in the story. Even though his house maybe looked nice, it fell to pieces when the storm came. Sometimes I act too quickly and make foolish decisions. Help me to be more thoughtful and careful in the future. I know You care for me - help me to care for others too. Amen.

READ IT IN THE BIBLE | MATTHEW 7:24–27

2. THE MAN WHO CLIMBED A TREE

When I was a little boy, I loved climbing trees. In the summertime, my brothers and I would climb trees as high as we could. I loved being near the top and gazing across the fields. It seemed as if we could see for miles!

In the Bible, we read about a man called Zacchaeus who climbed a Sycamore tree to see Jesus. He had to do this because he was very short and when everyone else lined up along the streets to see Jesus, he could not see over them!

We might have expected the people to let Zacchaeus stand at the front because he was short but no-one liked him and they refused to let him stand in front of them. People didn't like him because he was a thief and a liar!

Zacchaeus worked as a tax collector, so his job was to collect a certain amount of money from the people to pass onto the government. However, instead of asking them for the correct amount of money, he lied and told them they had to pay more and he kept the extra for himself.

Despite being very rich, Zacchaeus was not satisfied in life and was determined to see Jesus. So he had no choice but to climb up the tree and have a better view than everyone else. No one seemed to notice him

or even care that he was up there but when Jesus reached that spot, He stopped and looked up at Zacchaeus. Jesus, knowing how desperate Zacchaeus was to meet Him, told Zacchaeus to come down from the tree because He wanted to go to his house for tea!

Zacchaeus was probably so shocked that Jesus stopped to talk to him, he could have fallen out of the tree! No one else ever took time to speak to him but Jesus was interested in him. Everyone else was probably furious that Jesus talked to Zacchaeus and wondered if Jesus knew what kind of character he was. However, Jesus came to save everyone - good people as well as bad people.

Zacchaeus scrambled down from the tree and took Jesus to his house. That day, he became a Christian and his life was

changed forever. He told Jesus that he was going to give half of his possessions to the poor and if he had stolen from anyone he would return four times the amount!

Zacchaeus may not have changed on the outside - he was still a tax collector, however, he had changed on the inside. God forgave his sin and gave him a new clean heart. He was now a new man in Christ Jesus. This is what Jesus does to people - He changes them on the inside.

1. **Can climbing a tree make you a Christian?**

2. **Why did Zacchaeus climb a tree?**

3. **Why did the people not like Zacchaeus?**

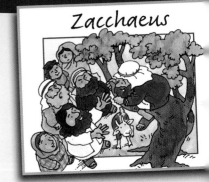

Zacchaeus

4. **How do we know Zacchaeus became a Christian? - How did he change?**

5. **How can we change when the Lord saves us?**

PRAYER...

Dear Father, this is a great story about someone who was small, yet who wanted to be tall so he could see You. Thank You for placing that tree right there for Zacchaeus to find. Thank You also for the determination he had to see You. Help me to be determined to know You just like Zacchaeus was. Thank You Lord for all the people You have saved. Please save many more. Amen.

| READ IT IN THE BIBLE | LUKE 19:1–10 |

3. THE BOY WITH THE NEW COAT

Have you ever gone shopping with your mum or dad to get a new coat? It is always exciting getting new clothes and wearing them for the first time. Most children enjoy putting on a team kit for playing sport, nice clothes for church or swimming gear for the beach.

Many girls, in particular, spend lots of time dressing up and trying on new clothes. From the youngest girl to an elderly grandmother, there is something special about dressing up. They spend hours deciding what to wear because many of them have gathered up lots of clothes over the years and have many combinations to choose from.

In this story, a young boy called Joseph was

given a new coat by his father, Jacob. The coat wasn't plain but was made up of many colours and Joseph loved it and wore it everywhere.

Joseph was the second youngest of Jacob's 12 sons and it seemed that Jacob loved Joseph more than the others. This made

Joseph's ten older brother[s] very jealous of him an[d] the special coat was [a] constant reminder t[o] them.

Instead of Joseph['s] brothers being happy for their little brother[s] they began to hat[e] the sight of him! Thi[s] is often how jealous[y] starts.

As time went on, the brothers let their hatred fester until one day they stripped Joseph of his coat and threw

him into a pit. They hoped a lion or bear might kill him but when that didn't happen, they sold him to a slave-trader who was going to Egypt, hundreds of miles away! Do you know who was with Joseph the whole time? The Lord! Isn't that wonderful?

Whenever a person we know gets something new, we should be happy for them and not be jealous. Being jealous is breaking one of God's Ten

13

Commandments. Number ten tells us 'Thou shalt not covet'. Coveting is desiring something that belongs to another person. Often we don't even need it but because we see someone else with it we think we do!

Although this is one of the saddest stories in the Bible, it has a happy ending because God took care of Joseph in Egypt and he became Prime Minister. Many years later, Joseph met his brothers and completely forgave them for their despicable actions. Often it is hard to forgive someone for mistreating us but that is what God asks us to do. After all, He sent His Son, Jesus, to die on the cross to forgive the sins of all who would trust in Him. Hence, Jesus is our perfect example of how we should forgive others. Therefore, we should ask God to help us forgive people who make fun of us or are jealous of us.

Sometimes, we can be jealous of others when they get new clothes or toys. We should be happy for them and focus on nice things that we already have and not pester our parents for the new things our friends have got.

14

It is interesting to note that God blessed Joseph in marvellous ways. Could this have been because he never fought with his brothers or responded in anger when they insulted him?

1. What are your favourite clothes to wear?

2. Why were Joseph's brothers jealous of him?

3. How can jealousy affect us?

4. Why is it so hard to forgive someone who wrongs us?

5. What should we do when we feel ourselves becoming jealous of someone?

PRAYER...

Dear Lord, thank You for all the clothes I have. I know there are many people in the world who have very few clothes to wear and I have so many I could even share mine with others. Thank You also for reminding me not to be selfish or jealous. It is so easy to want everything all the time even though I know I cannot have it. Help me to be content and happy for others who have better things than I do. Sometimes I feel myself getting angry, frustrated and even jealous of the smallest things. Help me not to be like that and help me to forgive others when I should. Please forgive me for all my bad thoughts. Amen.

READ IT IN THE BIBLE | GENESIS 37:1–36

4. Children love to play with water

I love to play with water. Whether it is having a water fight on a hot summer's day or swimming in the sea at the coast, I have great fun!

When I was a little child, I loved bath time as I splashed and played with the bubble bath foam! When it rained outside, I ran around and jumped in puddles - even though my mum always told me to walk around them! One day when I jumped so hard and soaked her, she chased me down the road! By the time she caught me I'm sure I'd said sorry a hundred times!

The Bible also mentions water on many occasions - let me share some of them with you. In Genesis, we read when God looked down on the world and saw it was full of wickedness, He destroyed it with a flood. The whole world was covered with water and only Noah and his family survived. God had

nstructed him to build an ark and nvite anyone who wanted to be saved o enter it. However, everyone else aughed at Noah and as a result they were drowned.

Around eight hundred years later we ead about Moses, the man God used o lead the children of Israel towards he Promised Land - all two million of hem! They had been living in Egypt for about four hundred years and were being treated harshly as slaves. After

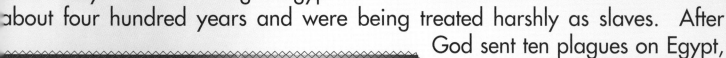

God sent ten plagues on Egypt, Pharaoh finally let the people go and Moses led them on a long journey until they came to the shores of the Red Sea.

By this time, Pharaoh had changed his mind and sent soldiers to capture the people again. Moses saw the soldiers approaching rapidly and prayed to God for help.

Suddenly, God divided the sec and made a path along the seabed to the far side. A huge wall of water went up on each side and Moses led the children of Israel across. By the time they reached the shore at the far side, the Egyptian army was crossing the seabed bu' God closed the sea and all o' them drowned that day. God was teaching the Egyptians not to be cruel to His children.

Then there was Naaman, a commander in an army, who had a disease called leprosy. In those times, there was no cure for it and it could be passed on to others. Even though Naaman had authority over many soldiers and had lots of money, nothing could take his leprosy away.

Then a little servant girl in his house told him that God could help him. He was so desperate to get healed, he agreed to visit God's prophet, Elisha. Elisha told him to dip in the River Jordan seven times and his leprosy

would be healed. Initially, he refused to do so because he was full of pride and would have felt embarrassed. Thankfully, Naaman's friend persuaded him that he had nothing to lose because he was going to die soon anyway. So he went and dipped in the River Jordan seven times and his leprosy left him! He recognised God had miraculously healed him and he trusted in God. Immediately, he told all his soldiers what the Lord had done for him.

Another famous story about water in the Bible is when a woman came to a well in Samaria to draw water. Jesus was sitting at the well and asked her for a drink. She asked Him why He spoke to her because no one else did. Jesus told her that He could give her water and she would never thirst again. He was talking about Himself because He is the 'Living Water' of life who offers us eternal satisfaction.

When the woman believed in Jesus, she immediately received

Encounter At Jacob's Well

the Living Water! She was so excited she told her whole village and they all came out to see Jesus. Over half of them became Christians that day when they also received Living Water - the Lord Jesus Christ.

Later in Jesus' ministry, one day when He was preaching He told people if they believed in Him the Holy Spirit would come into their lives. Then rivers of living water would flow out of them and other people would be refreshed by their joy and kindness as they told them about Jesus.

Water, like air, is one of the essential substances we need on earth to survive. Both air and water come from God - isn't God so kind? He knows exactly what our bodies need and all He asks in return is that we express our thanks to Him, especially His Son, Jesus - the Water of Life.

1. In what ways can you play with water?

2. Why is water so important?

3. Can you name three stories from the Bible with water in them?

4. Why did God destroy the world with a flood?

5. How is Jesus the Living Water?

PRAYER...

Dear Lord, thank You for all the amazing stories about water in the Bible. So often You provided water, even in the desert when people needed it most. Help me to be more grateful and thankful for the simple things in life, like water, and not take them for granted. I am continually amazed at Your kindness to us - we don't have to dig wells to get clean and fresh water like some people in other countries have to do. Thank You, Lord. Amen.

READ IT IN THE BIBLE — JOHN 4:5—42

5. Sticks in the Bible

What is it about children tho every time they walk throug a forest they want to pic up sticks? Maybe it is t

protect us from a wild animal or an intruder. For some reason, we often feel safe carrying a stick. My two favourite forest parks to explore are Hillsborough and Tollymore. When camping, I always gather up lots of sticks during the day to make a campfire to burn in the evenings for heat.

The Bible has lots of stories with sticks in them. Let me share some of them with you. Some of these stick stories also have animals in them.

One day God spoke to Moses in the form of a burning bush and asked him to go to Egypt to free the children of Israel from slavery. Moses didn't think the people would respect or listen to him so he began to make excuses as to why he should not go. God then told Moses to throw down the stick he had in his hand. As it hit the ground, it suddenly turned into a snake! Initially Moses ran away from it but God told him to pick it up by the tail. When Moses did so, it

changed back into a stick. God was showing Moses He is so powerful, He can do anything!

Many years later, another man of God called Elijah went to visit a widow who lived with her son. When Elijah arrived in her village, he found her outside gathering sticks to make a fire

so she could cook food for her son and herself. Shortly after Elijah arrived, her son became sick and died. Elijah prayed to God and asked Him to bring the boy back to life. God answered his prayer and Elijah presented the boy, alive and well, back to his mother! The mother was so touched she became a Christian. This was God's way of helping her believe.

Normally when someone dies, they do not come back to life. This story is a reminder that each of us can die at any time. It is not just old people who die, but many young people and even little children can die. This is why it is so important to believe in God and ask the Lord Jesus to forgive us for all our sins so we will spend eternity with God in Heaven when we die.

On another occasion, one of the students at Elisha's Bible school was chopping down a tree but the axe head flew off the axe and landed in the river. He cried out to Elisha for help as he had borrowed the axe and needed to return it to the owner. Elisha calmly threw a stick into the river at the place where the axe head landed and immediately it floated to the surface - this was a miracle.

In the New Testament, we read in the book of Acts that the Apostle Paul was shipwrecked just off the island of Malta. Thankfully, Paul and all the other passengers were able to swim safely to shore.

They were so cold they gathered sticks and lit a fire. As Paul set some sticks onto it, a snake jumped out of the fire and bit him on the arm. However, he was not harmed and did not die because God was protecting him.

The people who lived on the island were so amazed that many of them became believers in the Lord Jesus Christ. God can make any situation, no matter how bad, have a good outcome.

1. Why do children like to carry sticks when walking through the forest?

2. How can sticks be dangerous?

3. When Moses picked up a stick, can you remember what it turned into?

4. When Elijah visited the widow, what happened to her son?

5. What jumped out of the fire when Paul threw sticks onto it?

PRAYER...

Dear Lord, thank You for these amazing stories in the Bible about sticks. Some of them are connected with animals and I love animals. Sometimes playing with sticks can be dangerous so help me to be careful and not hurt anyone by accident. Also, please give me a desire to read the Bible more often so I can read more about how You cared for people who loved You. Amen.

READ IT IN THE BIBLE | 2 KINGS 6:1–7

6. Hide and Seek

This is my favourite game by far! As a child, I loved to play it with my brothers and even today I still love a good game of Hide-and-Seek, especially in the forest! When I was a little boy, I was able to hide in the smallest of places like in a wardrobe or under the bed and those looking for me didn't find me for ages!

Did you know that there are many stories of people who tried to play Hide-and-Seek in the Bible? Let me tell you about some of them.

The first one is in the Garden of Eden. A garden is a great place

HIDE AND SEEK

to hide, especially if there are lots of trees and bushes. However, on this occasion, it was very serious because it was God looking for Adam and Eve. They were trying to hide after disobeying Him. Isn't it amazing how when we do something wrong, we naturally want to hide or try to cover it up?

When God is looking for us, it is impossible to hide because God sees everything. In the Garden of Eden, God had previously instructed Adam and Eve not to eat from the tree in the middle of the garden. However, they rebelled against God and ate fruit that they had plucked from it. This was the first time humanity had sinned and because of their actions, sin came into the world. Their disobedience resulted in all their descendants being born in sin, with the need of a Saviour.

Isn't it true that whenever we are told not to touch something, we touch it? If we are told not to do something, we do it? When told not to look

at something, we look at it. This is called disobedience, which is a simple definition of sin. It is part of the nature we inherited at birth.

Another game of Hide-and-Seek took place between Elijah and an evil king called Ahab. The king told everyone they were no longer allowed to worship the one true God of Heaven but should worship an idol called Baal. Elijah challenged King Ahab over the matter but he refused to listen. Elijah then told King Ahab that there would be a drought across the land until he prayed and asked God to send rain again.

Just as Elijah claimed, God withheld the rain and very soon a famine arose. King Ahab became so angry he wanted to kill Elijah - but frustratingly he couldn't find him! That was because God hid Elijah next to a little river called Cherith. There, Elijah had plenty of fresh water to drink, and God also sent him bread and meat -

delivered by ravens! This game lasted for over two years and no one could find Elijah! God protected His servant because he stood up for the Lord and did what was right.

Another famous person in the Bible who played a long-lasting game of Hide-and-Seek was David - the shepherd boy who would later become king. After David killed the giant, Goliath, King Saul became really jealous of him and sent all his soldiers to hunt David down. David hid in forests, mountains and caves where no-one could find him. After a number of years, King Saul died and David was able to come out of hiding and take the throne. Jealousy is a terrible thing and often leads to hatred, lying and being frustrated.

In the New Testament, the Apostle Paul also got caught up in many games of Hide-and-Seek. Everywhere he went, people were hiding, lying in wait for him. In some places, the Christians hid in fear and were seeking for Paul to encourage them, while in other places, evil people were hiding to attack him. Hence Paul often had to hide for his own safety. Even when Paul was put in prison for preaching about Jesus, they were still seeking him so they could kill him. However, God

...helped him escape so he could preach elsewhere. Even today in some countries, it is dangerous to be a Christian. That is why we should never take following Jesus for granted. Every day we should thank God for how we can worship Him and pray freely.

1. **Why do we want to hide whenever we do something wrong?**

2. **When we are told not to touch something, why do we want to touch it?**

3. **When we do something we are told not to do, what is it called?**

4. **What is a Christian?**

5. **How does a person change whenever they become a Christian?**

PRAYER...

Dear Lord, I love playing Hide-and-Seek - it is so much fun! This story has taught me about Hide-and-Seek games in the Bible. Especially the first one when Adam and Eve tried to hide from You. They had sinned and knew their disobedience displeased You. Help me never to hide from You, Lord. I know I have sinned in the past and will sin in the future, even though I don't want to. Help me always be honest and tell the truth. It is hard at times but I know it is the right thing to do. In Jesus' name I pray, Amen.

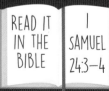

READ IT IN THE BIBLE | 1 SAMUEL 24:3–4

7. FRIENDS IN THE BIBLE

Having a true friend is one of the most wonderful things we can experience in the world. A friend is someone you can play, laugh and cry with. Most of all, they are someone you can trust with your life! I have made many friends over the years but sadly over time, some of them have moved on. However I always seem to make new ones for which I am very thankful.

It's better to have a few good friends who you can trust with your life rather than many acquaintances who wouldn't really miss you if you were gone.

The Bible talks about a friend who sticks closer than a brother. I have six brothers I am very close to but for a Christian, the Lord Jesus is an even closer friend than our nearest and dearest on earth.

David and Jonathan were best friends in the Bible. In fact, they were so close they made a promise to remain best friends for all of their lives. It was an unlikely friendship because Jonathan was the king's son and grew up in the palace - in contrast to David, who grew up looking after his father's sheep on the hills. However, they had a great respect for each other and even played and hunted together. Jonathan was next in line to the throne but realised that David would make a much better king than he would. He selflessly put his own aspirations to the side and told David he could take the throne instead.

When King Saul realised what was happening, he hated David with a passion and spent the rest of his life hunting him down. As a result, David had to flee and never saw Jonathan again.

Jonathan was eventuall[y] killed in battle and when th[e] news was brought to Davi[d] he wept many days for hi[s] friend because he love[d] him as much as he love[d] his own soul. David truste[d] Jonathan with his life an[d] proved it many times.

In the book of Esther, we read about a little orphan girl who was raised by he[r] older cousin, Mordecai. When Esther was older, Mordecai informed her th[at] the king was looking for a queen and suggested that she visit him. Esther wa[s] very excited and got her friends to style her hair and put on makeup to mak[e] her as beautiful as possible. There were many other girls also going to meet th[e] king and Esther wanted to make sure he would choose her over the rest of them to be his wife.

Whenever the king saw Esther, he saw that she was beautiful inside and out. He fell in love with her immediately and asked her to become his wife. Things went well at the start but after a few years there was a major

problem in the palace. Esther never panicked, but rather called her closest friends and asked them to pray for her. God answered their prayers and Esther became a hero for saving her people. A true friend is someone you can pray with as well as play with.

Daniel is another Bible hero who stood strong for God together with his friends. Daniel and his friends were tempted to compromise their beliefs in God. It started with their food when they were told to eat the king's meat and drink his wine - but they refused. God honoured them and made the four young men stronger and healthier looking than everyone else.

Whenever Daniel wasn't present, his three friends were told to bow down and worship a false god. They refused and subsequently were thrown into a fiery furnace. They were unharmed because the Angel of the Lord stood with them and protected them. Even when Daniel wasn't there, his friends remained strong and committed to their faith in God. They proved themselves to be good friends.

A few years later, other men who worked wit Daniel in the royal palace became jealous c him and tricked the king into throwing Danie into a lions' den. They hoped the lions woul eat him, but they didn't realise that Daniel God would be with him in the den and prever the lions from causing him any harm. The nex morning, the king had Daniel lifted out of th den to safety. However, the king was furiou with the cowardly men who had tricked hir and he had them thrown into the den immediately as punishment! Althoug minutes earlier, the lions had been peacefully lying beside Daniel, they gobble up the evil men before they even reached the bottom of the den! Daniel is great example to Christians today because he prayed with his friends when the were together, but when they were separated, he took time alone to pray fo them. Most of all, God was his best friend and he never forgot that!

In the New Testament, Paul and Barnabas were really good friends. Even when no one else wanted Paul in their company, Barnabas stood up for him and told them he was a good friend. Barnabas was a great encouragement to Paul and kept him going on strong for God when situations were difficult. It is important to encourage your friends by finding

omething positive about them and complimenting them on it. As you get older you will find many people will try to discourage you. Try not to be affected by their remarks and more importantly do not become one of those people!

Later on, Paul and Barnabas disagreed over an issue and went their separate ways. No doubt it was sad for both of them, yet each of them kept going on for God. Try to choose friends who help you stay close to God and seek to live their own lives pleasing to Him.

1. How would you describe what a friend is?

2. Who are your best friends?

3. What is a true friend?

4. How can Jesus be our best friend?

5. If our friends are mean to us, what should we do?

PRAYER...

Dear Lord, thank You for the friends I have. Good friends are often hard to find. Help me to be friendly because I know it says in the Bible that if we want to have friends, we must show ourselves to be friendly. Thank You for being the best friend that anyone can ever have. You even promise that You will never leave me nor forsake me. Please never let me forget how much You love me and care for me. In Jesus' name I pray, Amen.

READ IT IN THE BIBLE | DANIEL 1:1—6

8. Run Run Run

Running is, without doubt, the most common sport in the world. Nearly all popular sports in the world involve running to some degree. From the moment children can walk, they begin to run, and run and run!

When I was younger, I used to love running. I grew up on a farm and ran everywhere while feeding the animals and doing my chores. For me, it was a challenge to get as much done as possible each day. When I was a teenager, Sports Day was my favourite day of the school year. I also represented my school at regional races competing against other boys from all across the country.

The Bible has many stories about people running. It even refers to animals, such as pigs and bears running! The fastest runner of them all was the prophet, Elijah. He was so fast he was able to outrun King Ahab's horse that was bringing the king back to the palace!

As well as being a great sprinter, Elijah was also able to run long distances. Shortly after outrunning King Ahab's horse, he ran over a hundred miles - in fear for his life. He finally stopped and sat under a tree in the middle of the desert. He was very discouraged and wanted to give up on life. However, God sent an angel to him with food and water to restore his body. The angel asked him why he wanted to give up. Elijah told the angel that he was the only believer who didn't bow down to the false god, Baal. The angel informed Elijah that there were actually seven thousand other people who trusted in the one true God and had not bowed down to Ahab's idol. This really encouraged Elijah and after a short rest, he went back and found the people who served God.

Another person who the Bible tells us loved to run was Samuel. When he was just a little boy, one night the Lord called him four times while he was sleeping. The first three times, he jumped out of bed and ran to Eli, the priest, and asked him why he was calling him! Initially, Eli thought that Samuel was dreaming, but then he realised God was

calling Samuel. Eli told Samuel, the next time he heard the voice, he was to invite God to speak to him as he lay in his bed. God then called Samuel a fourth time and gave Samuel a very important message about Eli and his two sons.

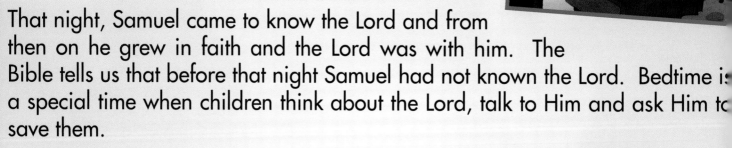

That night, Samuel came to know the Lord and from then on he grew in faith and the Lord was with him. The Bible tells us that before that night Samuel had not known the Lord. Bedtime is a special time when children think about the Lord, talk to Him and ask Him to save them.

Another Bible character who loved to run was David - the shepherd boy who later became king. While he worked in the fields caring for his father's sheep, there were occasions when he ran after bears and lions who crept up and grabbed one of his lambs in their mouths! When he was a little older, the nation of Israel was at war with their greatest enemy, the Philistines. One of the Philistine soldiers was a giant called Goliath and no

one from Israel dared to fight him. However, when David heard Goliath defy God, he fearlessly offered to fight the giant and defeated him with a single slingshot! The entire Philistine army turned and fled in fear and Israel had peace for many years!

Despite David winning this battle to free Israel, King Saul became jealous of David and tried to kill him! David had to flee and ran for many months and years to avoid King Saul's soldiers who were seeking him. During this time on the run, David formed his own army with over six hundred men. Some of them were fiercer than lions and were swifter than deer!

In the New Testament, Philip, one of the men appointed to serve in the newly-formed church in Jerusalem, was instructed by an angel to make a journey south into the desert. Philip obeyed and when he got there, the Holy Spirit told him to speak to a man from

Ethiopia who was sitting in a chariot reading his Bible Philip ran over to him and explained that the person he was reading about was Jesus. The man became a Christian that day and was baptised immediately in a nearby pool of water.

Whenever the disciples, Peter and John heard that Jesus had risen from the dead and his tomb was empty, both of them ran to see for themselves. John was faster and got there before Peter!

Some years later, Peter was put in prison for being a Christian. His friends gathered together to pray for him and while they were praying God sent an angel to help Peter escape! Once outside the prison, Peter, immediately went to the house where everyone was praying. He knocked the door and a little girl answered. When she saw it was Peter she was so excited that she ran through the house to tell everyone. They all thought she was mad until Peter made himself known. God answered their prayer even while they were still praying!

1. Describe why children often run rather than walk?

2. Name three stories in the Bible where we read of people running?

3. How many times did God call Samuel?

4. Why did the people think the little girl was mad?

5. How can we run for Jesus?

PRAYER...

Dear Lord, thank You so much for my legs that help me to walk and run. Every morning I wake up I just want to run, run and run! I am so glad I can do this and often I forget to thank You for my healthy body. With my legs, I can kick a ball, skip and even ride a bike. These people in the Bible loved to run for You - help me to do the same. I know it takes a lot of energy to run, so help me use lots of my energy to live for You. I also know I need to rest and that is why I have a bed. Help me to stop running now so I can get a good sleep because I know tomorrow, the moment I wake up, my legs will want to start running even though my eyes might want to go back to sleep! Amen.

READ IT IN THE BIBLE — 1ST KINGS 19:1-9

9. CHILDREN LOVE TO BUILD HOUSES

Nearly all children have tried to build a house at some stage! I remember as a little boy, I used to love building houses with my brothers. In the living room, we used chairs as walls and then used a blanket to make a roof. Sometimes, a huge cardboard box made a great house and we cut out windows and made a door.

In the summertime, we often made huts out of hay which looked like little houses. In primary school, one of my favourite games was playing 'house' with the other kids.

In the Bible, we read how various people had all kinds of homes and lived in different types of houses. Remember a house is just a building, but it is the people who live in it that make it a home. Houses can be made out of many things such as bricks, blocks, wood, mud or clay. Some have stairs, while other's don't.

In the beginning, God gave Adam and Eve a beautiful home in the Garden of Eden - imagine how amazing it would have been living there. Then we read about Abraham and how for most of his life, he lived in a tent and travelled from one place to another. Many people in the Bible lived like this as they had to move around with their animals to make sure they had grass to eat and water to drink.

Joseph had a comfortable upbringing in his father, Jacob's house. However, after his jealous brothers sold him as a slave, he ended up spending many years living in prison, for a crime he didn't commit!

Later on in the Bible, we read how David lived in many places. When he was young, he spent many nights under the trees looking after his father's sheep. Then when King Saul sought to kill him, David spent many months on the run, living in forests and caves. Later, after King Saul's death, David became the king and lived in the royal palace.

There is also a story in the Bible about a couple who built an extension onto their house to make a room for the prophet Elisha to stay in any time he was passing by. In it, they put a bed, a lamp and a table. Around this time, Elisha had a number of students wanting to learn more about God. They decided to build a Bible College out of wood so they went to the forest and cut down trees to use in the construction.

There were also many kings and queens in the Bible that lived in luxurious palaces. These were substantial, beautiful buildings. Boys and girls born in the palaces were princes and princesses. We also read how a little orphan girl called Esther married a king and moved into the palace. In contrast, Moses spent the first 40 years of his life in Pharaoh's palace in Egypt but then lived in the wilderness the rest of his life! In the latter part of Moses' life, he led two million Israelites around the desert. As they moved around there was a special tent called the Tabernacle, which was where the people came to worship God.

Later, when the people entered the Promised Land, they replaced the Tabernacle with a permanent building called the Temple. Often the priests lived in the Temple and that is where the little boy Samuel grew up.

One of the most exciting types of houses God talks about in the Bible are mansions. God prepares mansions in Heaven for people who believe in Him and become Christians.

A Christian is anyone who believes in Jesus Christ and trusts Him to be their Saviour. After dying, they will immediately go to Heaven to be with the Lord Jesus and all the other Christians who have died before them. Jesus told His disciples He was returning to Heaven to prepare mansions there for each of His children. When He finishes this work, He will return to earth to bring all His children home to Heaven. I am really looking forward to that day!

1. Can you name some items you can make a house from?

2. Can you name five types of houses that people in the Bible had?

3. Why did Abraham keep moving around with his tent?

4. What type of home is the Lord Jesus preparing in heaven for Christians?

5. If someone wanted to be sure of having a mansion in Heaven, what must they do?

PRAYER...

Dear Lord, thank You for my house and home. I know some children in the world don't have nice houses; in fact, some don't have anywhere to sleep. I also pray for all the orphans in the world who live in an orphanage and have no one to love them. One day when I grow up, I will want to live in a house. Please make it be a home that is full of love, which is more important than a fancy house without love. Help me to appreciate everything I have and never complain about the things I don't have. Amen.

READ IT IN THE BIBLE | 2ND KINGS 4:8–10

10. Children love to play music

Children all over the world love music. When little babies hear music, they wriggle and smile. When young children hear music, they want to jump and dance around and teenagers find it entertaining and relaxing. Even older people listen to music and tap their feet along to the beat.

Many children are musical and learn to play musical instruments like the piano, flute and recorder. Others love to sing in their school or church choirs. When I visit schools to conduct Bible Clubs, I find children love to sing and are naturally very good at it.

When I was a little boy, I was asked to join the school choir. After the first song, the teacher asked me to make the actions with my mouth but not to make any noise. It felt like I was stretching my mouth. For a long time, I couldn't understand until a friend told me I was too loud and out of tune!

The Bible also has lots to say about musical instruments and singing praises to the Lord. It is natural for people to want to express worship in the form of praise to someone or something; this is why we worship God. He desires that we worship Him and loves it when we sing His praises. In the New Testament, the church is instructed to praise God with Psalms, hymns and spiritual songs. Many musical instruments are found in the Bible - the harp, violin, pipes, trumpet and cymbals are all mentioned.

Throughout the Bible, we read about God's people singing praises to Him and playing musical instruments. We read in Genesis, they played the pipes and in Exodus they sang, danced and played the tambourine. Moses and David were

responsible for writing most of the songs contained in the Bible. David, known as 'the Sweet Psalmist of Israel' is credited with writing about half of the 150 songs recorded in Psalms, as well as some in the historical books.

Music was also used on special occasions, such as royal coronations and special feasts. Trumpets sounded when the walls of Jericho fell down and David played his harp to soothe Saul when he was depressed.

Two of the Gospels mention the fact that Jesus and His disciples sang a hymn at the end of the Last Supper. Elsewhere in the Gospels, music was used at times of mourning and celebration. The Bible says if anyone is happy or cheerful, let them sing praises. God loves it when we sing to Him or play a musical instrument to praise His name.

In his New Testament letters, the Apostle Paul instructed the Christians in the towns of Corinth and Colossae to do everything in life as if it were unto the Lord. This includes when we sing or play music to praise God.

1. Who is the person we should sing to more than anyone else?

2. Does the Bible mention music a little or a lot?

3. Name at least three musical instruments in the Bible?

4. Which two men wrote most of the songs in the Bible?

5. Does God like it when we sing to Him?

PRAYER...

Dear Lord, I just love to praise Your name. Every time I sing, I think about how You are such a wonderful, amazing and awesome God. You deserve all our praise and I love to praise You with my lips. Help me when I am singing to sing with all my heart. If I ever learn to play a musical instrument, help me to play it well and most of all to praise and worship You with any talent You have given me. Thank You so much Lord for who You are. I am so small and You are so big, yet You know everything about me. Thank You Lord, Amen.

READ IT IN THE BIBLE — EPHESIANS 5:19

11. CHILDREN LOVE BIRDS

Birds are fascinating creatures created by God that come in many shapes, sizes and colours. Think about the pretty little birds that visit your garden - like the Robin, Sparrow, Greenfinch and Blue Tit. When we go to the coast, we often see and hear Seagulls high up in the cliffs. Then in cities, there always seems to be lots of Pigeons about. As a child, I loved to chase Pigeons down the street and see if I could catch one! Then there are enormous birds of prey, like the Eagle, Hawk and Vulture.

BIRD SOUNDS

Birds are intelligent creatures and know the times and seasons. Their instinct tells them when to migrate to warmer climates in the autumn, and then return before it gets too hot there! Unlike us humans, they never get lost when travelling!

The Bible mentions birds a lot and God refers to them frequently. Over three hundred verses in the Bible mention birds in some context.

While Noah was in the ark, he let out two birds - a Raven and a Dove - to see if there was any sign of land for the birds to rest on. The Raven didn't return to the ark because it was happy to eat dead flesh, but the Dove couldn't find land to set its feet on, so it returned several times until the trees were visible for it to sit on.

I Kings 17:6

The ravens brought him bread and meat in the morning, and bread and meat in the evening; and he drank from the brook.

The Ravens were mentioned again whenever Elijah was hiding from the evil King Ahab by the river. Ravens brought him fresh bread and meat every day. This is amazing considering they are scavenger birds who would normally eat the bread themselves.

The Eagle is a huge bird and is so strong it can fly high into the sky where it is beyond danger and can see everything. When a person becomes a Christian, God wants them to be strong like an Eagle. When worries, problems and difficulties come their way, they should rise above them and keep soaring for Christ.

To the other extreme, Jesus often talked about one of the smallest birds, the little sparrow. He said that whenever a Sparrow falls to the ground, God knows all about it. Most people would never notice it or care, but God is interested. Jesus continued the lesson and told the people if any of them were His children, think how much more He cared for them! In comparison to many other brightly-coloured birds, sparrows are just a dull brown or grey. Yet God encourages us that even though we might not be as pretty, smart or strong as others might be, He still cares for us and loves us exactly the same.

Not long before His death, Jesus stood and wept as He gazed over the great city of Jerusalem. He loved the people so much He was going to die to save them, even though most of them weren't interested

in Him. He used the illustration of a mother hen gathering her chicks under her wings to describe how He wished that people would run to Him for salvation. Instead, the people rejected Him and had Him crucified a short time later.

1. Can you name at least four types of birds?

2. Which birds fed Elijah with bread and meat?

3. Which bird does God know all about when it falls to the ground?

4. What have you learned about the Eagle today?

5. Why did Jesus cry in Jerusalem?

PRAYER...

Dear Lord, what fascinating lessons there are to learn about birds - little ones and big ones. Thank You for making them so pretty and giving them feathers to keep them warm and wings to make them fly. It's amazing how the Ravens listened to You when You told them to feed Elijah in the desert. They could have eaten his food but they didn't. Help me to appreciate all the animals and birds You created and placed in this world. Thank You again for teaching me more about Your creation. In Jesus' name I pray, Amen.

READ IT IN THE BIBLE | MATTHEW 10:29—31

12. Children love to play with their hair

I am not so familiar with this subject because I don't have much hair! It seemed like one morning I woke up and all my hair was gone! I checked under my pillow and under my bed but couldn't find it - it was gone forever! But nonetheless, boys, girls, men and women all love their hair.

When people walk past a mirror, nearly everyone will stop and look at their hair and more often than not, adjust it with their fingertips! For a long time, I thought women took lots of selfies with their phone until one day I realised they were just using their phone camera as a mirror to make sure their hair was sitting nicely!

The Bible also mentions hair and beauty in several places. When Esther was going to meet the king, she spent a long time with her friends trying to make herself look as pretty as possible. I am sure her friends spent a lot of time brushing and styling her hair. The Bible tells us that a woman's hair is her glory.

There is a very interesting story in the Bible about a man called Samson. Samson's birth was announced by an angel at a time when Israel was being ruled by their enemies, the Philistines. Samson was born a Nazarite and was set apart with supernatural strength from God. On one occasion, the Philistines made fun of him and he killed one thousand men with the jaw bone of a donkey!

The Philistines then took Samson's wife and got her to marry another man. This made Samson really angry so he caught three hundred foxes, and tied their tails together and set them on fire! Then he released them and they ran through the Philistines' fields and burned their crops.

Samson then fell in love with a beautiful Philistine woman named Delilah. The Philistine rulers came to Delilah and offered her money if she found out what made Samson so strong. Delilah went home and made a great meal for Samson and asked him what made him so strong.

Samson told her if he was bound with seven new bowstrings that had not been dried, he would lose his strength. Delilah went and told the rulers and the next time Samson was asleep, Delilah bound him up with the ropes. To Delilah's surprise, Samson had tricked her and when he awoke, he was able to break free. The next time she asked the same question, Samson told her he would lose his strength if he was tied up with brand new ropes that had never been used. Delilah again tried to trap Samson while he slept, but just like before, he was able to break free. Delilah was very hurt by Samson telling her lies and questioned his love for her since he could not share the secret to his strength.

The next day, Delilah asked Samson again and again about his strength and finally he told her the secret - how he was given his strength at birth by God, but if his hair was cut he would lose it. That evening as Samson slept, Delilah cut off his hair and called in the Philistines. The Philistine men then barged in and were able to capture Samson as his exceptional strength had gone. The Philistines gouged out his eyes and blinded him and put him in a prison in Gaza.

Sometime later, the Philistines were having a great festival and decided to bring Samson out before the crowd of rulers and people to mock him and celebrate his capture. Samson's hair had begun to grow back and as he leaned against the pillars of the huge building, he prayed that God would give him strength once more to defeat the Philistines. Samson used all of his might and pushed the pillars so hard that the roof came crashing down, killing himself and thousands of Philistines - Israel's cruel enemy.

Despite Samson making many bad decisions in life, God was still willing to forgive him and used Samson to accomplish many great things. It was through Samson's destruction of the Philistine pagan temple at his death that the Israelites were freed from Philistine rule.

1. What was the secret of Samson's strength?

2. How many Philistines did Samson kill with the jawbone of a donkey?

3. How did Samson's wife trick him?

4. Why did Delilah take money to sell Samson's secret?

5. Did God forgive Samson for what he did?

6. What final thing did Samson do to free his own people?

PRAYER...

Dear Lord, this has been an interesting story about Samson and his hair. I would never have guessed the secret of his strength was his long hair. He obviously had a very quick temper and couldn't control it at times. Help me not to get angry easily and when I do, help me to keep it under control. History is very important and it amazes me how You raised up this one man, Samson, to free Your people from the Philistines. Thank You for the freedom we have to live, sleep and most of all, worship You. In Jesus' name I pray, Amen.

READ IT IN THE BIBLE | JUDGES 16:16-17